THE CARS

THE

CARS

PHOTOGRAPHS BY PHILIP KAMIN
TEXT BY PETER GODDARD

McGRAW-HILL BOOK COMPANY
New York St. Louis San Francisco Auckland Bogotá Guatemala
Hamburg Johannesburg Lisbon London Madrid Mexico Montreal
New Delhi Panama Paris San Juan São Paulo
Singapore Sydney Tokyo Toronto

1 2 3 4 5 6 7 8 9   8 7 6

ISBN 0-07-033498-6

LIBRARY OF CONGRESS CATALOGING-IN-PUBLICATION DATA

Kamin, Philip.
The Cars.
1. Cars (Musical group) — Iconography.   2. Rock
musicians — United States — Iconography.   I. Title.
ML421.C3K35 1986   784.5'4'00922   85-19917
ISBN 0-07-033498-6 (pbk.)

Designed by Keith Abraham, ATA, Toronto.

For Seiichi and Mitsuka

Very special thanks to The Cars, Steve Berkowitz, Julia, Jeff, Elliot Roberts and
especially Ben Orr, for their friendship, help, and cooperation.
Special thanks to Bernie Kamin, Madeleine Morel, Glenda Herro, Tom Miller,
and Tom Dembofsky.
Thanks also to Leo Robichaud, Doug Paddey, Marty Ingles, and Gary Beck
at Canon Cameras of Canada.

Philip Kamin

Contents

OPPOSITE: Ben Orr and Ric Ocasek at Worcester.

Prologue

The Cars are among rock's leading riddles. As far as I can tell, there is no real reason for this. They are, after all, quite public. They tour. Their albums sell in the millions — many millions. They have hit singles. Their pictures show up in your local newspapers from time to time. Their videos are sleek, well tooled, neat and oft-played. The Cars like to talk. They like to discuss ideas. They like to argue. Critics, for the most part, seem to like them. And they're fairly visible around hometown Boston.

Still, what are they like? What do they look like? Okay, Ric Ocasek, gaunt face, his eyes hidden behind dark glasses, has what the music biz these days calls an ''image.'' But even here things get fuzzy. What exactly is Ocasek all about? What is this image? And what about the others, especially now that they've all come up with projects outside of the Cars?

Rock, despite all its up-front, physical qualities, can also be a shadow game, a play of mysteries, of clues behind clues. This is particularly true of the kind of rock which uses words and uses them well. The Cars use words extremely well. These are Ric Ocasek's words and, if you are inclined to let them, they can draw you into the music — and into further questions about what the music means and who, exactly, are the men behind it.

But you probably know something of this if you've gone this far. We're here not to create further mysteries, but to unravel some of them, and there's no better way than the most direct way — the Cars in pictures.

There's more here than what appears on the surface.

1 Out In Front

"Right from the start, we've never done anything exactly the way other bands might have done it."

David Robinson

The Cars are dining out. With a critic. The Cars are hungry; the critic is nervous.

Sushi.

They're *attacking* this sushi. The critic, invited by the local branch manager of the local branch of the local distributor of the band's record company, is not so sure of what to do. "Talk to them over dinner," he's been told. "Don't worry, they'll like you."

Well, the critic's not so sure. Are they even aware he's here? he wonders. Worse, if they are aware he's here, do they also know he's a critic? He thinks frantically about what he's said about the Cars. Jeez, nothing negative, he hopes. He thinks about ordering in. Pizza maybe.

He's nervous about what to say or ask. No problem. The band likes to talk. They've just finished another lightning-fast brief tour of bigger and bigger halls. "Oh, we talk about playing smaller places all the time," says Greg Hawkes, the very intent keyboard player. "But that's all we do — talk."

This, the critic thinks, is not going to be easy. This is a band still in evolution. This is a band that will always be evolving.

Within a year of their first recording in 1977, they'd signed with a major

Ben and David celebrating Ben's eighteenth birthday.

Elliot Easton — looking like Brian Jones.

record label. Before the next year had finished, they had their first major hit, "My Best Friend's Girl." The following year they'd copped every award imaginable as Band of the Year. When their second album, *Candy-O*, was released in June 1979 (with its coolly sensuous Alberto Vargas cover of a red-headed woman slumbering in a sheer black, skin-tight shift on the hood of a car), more than 600 radio stations immediately started playing it.

Even here, at the table ballooning with plates of Japanese delicacies, the critic scrambled for a name to describe their style. There were only a couple of things he felt sure of, he figured. The Cars had become the great singles band of the new music. The 1984 album, *Heartbeat City*, alone had been a reservoir of pop single hits. Another thing: they'd become one of the very few bands to compete directly with the British new wave. As with the first one in the early 60s, many of the new American bands mirrored the British sound. Each city worth its own alternative scene had its Sex Pistols and its own Sid Vicious. The Cars had recorded their debut album at AIR Studio in London, in February 1978, with Roy Thomson Baker who they found "ripping, to say the least." But still, it was a very American album. Maybe being expatriates, for however brief a time the band had been in London, had sharpened their instincts for America.

Anyway, it had worked. It had worked quietly, though, in a way that was almost unnoticed by much of the rock press. The Cars had picked up speed first on AM radio, not FM. They had hit singles, not just hit albums. Their audience had in it young kids whose very *first* record was a Cars record. These Cars had driven into that critical no-man's land where the Guess Who, Creedence Clearwater Revival and a few others had gone before; they'd become enormously popular, their music had gained considerable respect, yet they'd not become part of the rock 'n' roll fashion *hip* parade. They were getting inside the imagination of rock's new audience, but they were still outsiders to rock's establishment.

But there was the mood for change. And everywhere could be found Carclones; bands new and old and unmentionably bad, copying the band's neat, discrete, unsentimental sound. The Cars individually were passing their ideas, if not their style, on to a number of Boston-based bands. And yet, with all this information at his fingertips, with news coming in almost daily about this band out of Boston which was quickly becoming the band of its time, an appalling thought struck me.

I hadn't a clue as to what they were up to.

And I knew they were up to something.

But what?

I looked around the table. Ben Orr had the great, heavy lidded, sullen-eyed look of lead singers at their best. Hawkes wasn't the silent automan he sometimes seemed on stage, the robotic kid scientist behind a wall of keyboards and electronic gizmos; he seemed restless and questioning. Elliot Easton was perhaps the hardest to figure out. His reputation as one of the new music's master guitarists had taken little time to reach the public, coming as it had from other guitarists who'd been watching, or rather *listening*, to him. It was a reputation not based on the flash and filigree most guitar players use to carve out a niche for themselves — those huge, plunging solos meant to bowl you over. His reputation, instead, came from what you often *didn't* hear, the notes he didn't play, the clever spaces and silences he left in a line or phrase. He seemed impatient. He didn't like small talk.

Ric Ocasek, I noticed, was like a band within the band. He wasn't distant from the others — far from it, in fact, but he had his own dynamic. I remembered something he'd said, though, about writing a song in such a way so that it could seem to mean one thing one day and another thing the next.

Elliot with then co-manager Steve Berkowitz and Doug Sahm of the Sir Douglas Quintet.

"The ambiguity should be preserved," was Ocasek's line. It described him, in a way.

Then there was David Robinson. If the Cars were a movie, Robinson would be its cautious, soft-spoken hero — its Gary Cooper. He seemed so amiable and slow to anger, yet it was easy to forget that he'd been quick to help streamline these Cars — helped shape their image and style.

"Right from the start," Robinson said as he leaned across the table toward the critic, "we've never done anything exactly the way other bands might have done it. And that seems to be the source of some of the negative things we hear about the band — that we *are* unconventional in the way we record or talk to the press or whatever. It's odd hearing about anyone who is trying to be un-conventional, like us."

Unconventional, indeed. First there was that critic in England, Robinson went on, who was not impressed by the new American music coming from the Cars. "He didn't like anything about us, even our album covers. He said we should quit."

Robinson had been particularly stung by this knock. After all, he had been the one who had coaxed pin-up painter extraordinaire, Alberto Vargas, out of retirement to do the *Candy-O* cover. He was the one who designed the cover for *Panorama*. He looked intently at the critic, and I thought about looking intently for the exit. But Robinson smiled and went on.

"There's another way things happen to us that don't happen to other bands — or audiences. I find our audiences are getting younger. It should be the other way around. I'm getting mobbed by kids ten, twelve years old.

"It used to be I was never recognized. But I am now."

2 Ric Ocasek

They say T.S. Eliot liked *My Fair Lady* better than he liked the George Bernard Shaw original, *Pygmalion.* This shocks all sorts of academics out there who wonder how the poet who could write ''Winter kept us warm, covering/Earth in forgetful snow'' could *possibly* appreciate a *My Fair Lady*-ism such as ''Arabs learn Arabian with the speed of summer lightning.'' Actually, it makes sense to me as it did to Eliot, I assume. More than the meaning of the words is involved with *My Fair Lady's* poetry (or near poetry or whatever you want to call it). The words' relationship to their musical environment is obviously crucial — how words work as sound and how sound in turn adds meaning to words. But something else is involved here, something Ric Ocasek knows about words and music. He's said he doesn't know what poetry is. He's maintained that he doesn't understand how poetry's forms, sonnets and the like, work. What he *does* know is how a word disappears into the meaning it's meant to create. Back in the days of Cap'n Swing, and even before, he was reading poets such as Ferlinghetti and writing lower case poems à la e.e. cummings. (Some fans who knew him then still have copies of the collection of poems he published, all with the look of cummings' work.) But the Cars presented unique opportunities for a poet who had new forms for poetry on his mind.

In a Ric Ocasek poem, life is forever sneaking up on the poet's romance to nip at its ankles. In a Ric Ocasek song, the singer can be both hero and fall guy. Ben Orr's voice becomes the perfect straight man for the low blow coming from the lyrics. Or, as he explains about that early tune, ''Good Times Roll,'' ''It's not really about 'good times' at all. Actually, it's about paying for things twice and not knowing it.''

''I'm a test pilot for mass hysteria,'' he's said.

He's a ''stenographer for the masses,'' he's also said.

Ocasek grew up in Baltimore, went to a Catholic school, learned lots about guilt, sin and retribution, and found solace in hanging out with street gangs. The story goes that it was hearing the Crickets' ''That'll Be The Day'' that fueled his interest in music. Nothing was firing up his interest in his studies, though, until the family moved to Cleveland and he was nearly finished high school; he had to figure out what he was going to do with his life. His university career, at Antioch and Bowling Green, proved to be shortlived, and it was back to Cleveland with his guitar and his head full of lyrics — and a chance meeting in Columbus, Ohio, with Ben Orr at a party one night.

Ocasek and Orr may have looked like rock's odd couple, one tall and dark, the other short and blond, but their ideas blended. They played together in Ann

Arbor and Indianapolis and Cleveland and...well, not getting anywhere, they headed east in 1973 and landed in the middle of Harvard Square. Ocasek figures he had $100 at the time. Soon enough, he and Orr started putting bands together. Milkwood, an early folk effort, actually recorded an album for Paramount. Next came a band named for them by a local hero, Jonathon Richman: Richard and the Rabbits. Here they met Greg Hawkes. But then it was back to being Ocasek and Orr, folk duo, doing the local circuit, working at The Idler and the Inn Square.

Their meeting with Greg Hawkes led them to put together Cap'n Swing, with Elliot Easton added to the lineup. It was the good Cap'n's early songs that found their way onto the few local radio stations, WCOZ and WBCN, which supported local bands. Boston bands in the early 70s, if less involved in the brave new trends that New York bands were, had a certain passion you couldn't find elsewhere. The fiasco of the ''Boss-Town Sound'' hype by one record company in the 60s as the answer to San Francisco's growing scene was not a mistake of geography but of artistic judgment — the wrong bands being signed for the wrong reasons. Boston, Ocasek found, was deep in good musicians.

One deejay who played Cap'n Swing on her show was Maxanne Sartori, who had the afternoon shift on WBCN-FM. ''I saw them play live before I'd heard any tapes,'' she remembers. ''They reminded me of a weird combination of Velvet Underground, Roxy Music and Steely Dan. I flipped out. I started going to every gig they played. And I became friendly with Ric. He started asking me for advice because I used to live with someone in Boston who was a struggling rock and roller and who now is pretty successful. His name is Billy Squier. Ric knew Billy, and Ric thought maybe I had some sort of answers other people around town didn't have — Boston is not known as a management town. He thought of me managing them, but I turned it down because I told them I couldn't do anything for them. The funniest thing about meeting Ric was that I'd gone to the same college as he had at the time — Antioch.''

Cap'n Swing was hot enough to earn a shot at the big time — a gig in front of various record and management companies in New York. ''After they bombed there,'' Maxanne continues, ''I told Ben he's got to have something in his hands. He used to be a lead singer without any instrument. And he's probably the most photogenic of anyone in the band, but he didn't look comfortable on the stage at that time. He just looked foolish standing out there with nothing to do with his hands and nothing to do with his feet. So I said, 'What does he play?' And Ric said, 'He plays a lot of things — he can play anything.' So then I asked, 'What does he play best?' 'Probably the bass,' was the answer. 'Well, tell him he's got to play the bass from now on.'

''Anyway, the first time I noticed they had a mass following was when I was working for Mink DeVille, doing promotion for them, and we went to Boston where he was playing three nights at The Rat.''

The Rat was *the* Boston bar that mattered. Bands that mattered, DMZ and the like, were Rat bands. Sartori, of course, knew that, having featured many bands on her radio show. She recalls those three nights: ''We were smart enough to have the Cars open for us. I went to the gig the first night, and I was expecting a lot of people there. But there were 600, 700 people waiting in line, around the block, in the Fenway area, and for a club which could only hold 300 people. And it wasn't just because of Mink DeVille. These people loved the Cars.

''I was being considered for an A&R job with a record company and I brought one of the company's guys over to The Rat to hear them. He said he thought they were horrible on stage. 'Well,' I told him, 'I don't think that matters in selling records.' ''

Not, as it turned out, Cars records. Ocasek, among other things, writes

OPPOSITE: Ric lounging outside a Boston studio.

16

anti-romantic songs about romance. And David Robinson, the drummer, found them a bit mystifying at first. But during the winter of 1976-77 that they spent in Ocasek's basement, they took the words off the page and put them into sound.

"I think there are two kinds of music on our records," Ocasek told me. "There's the music that's very accessible and the stuff that isn't so accessible. And the contrast between the two is very interesting. There's always a split there. This is different for a band that's got mass appeal. This is not a band that is as far out as Psychic TV, but it definitely does give you something more to think about than just your normal pop genre kind of music."

Ric's attraction to Andy Warhol, who shot the band's video "Hello Again," comes from the similarity between Warhol's sense of what work is all about and Ocasek's sense of what his writing is all about. "Andy's always had this quirky view of everything. He's got a neat sensibility about things and he's usually off-the-cuff with his ideas. Through the years I've always been a fan of his because I think he's an important artist and I think he's spearheaded the pop-art movement. I think he's in for criticism because he's new and inventive, but a hundred years down the line Andy's stuff will still be around.

"He paints the things that are prevalent in his time. He paints what surrounds us now. That's what pop is. Pop music does the same thing. It talks about what surrounds us now. He did a few portraits of me a few years back and I've been going to [Warhol's] the Factory and seeing what he's up to.

"And I flashed on his old films, those old things and I thought, 'Why should all rock videos be so high-tech and perfect? Let's see if we can maybe do a lot on eight-millimeter.' We'd just done a very high-tech video, 'You Might Think,' something very state-of-the-art, and I thought we might get away from that approach. I'd also seen a show of Andy's in New York which was basically on fashion and interviews, but it was the same as his artwork, his way of framing things, his colors, just the way he looks at things. So I thought it would be a good idea for him to do a video with us. We did a lot on eight-millimeter. There are two versions of it, a long and a short version, but it's the same song, 'Hello Again.' It's different."

3 Early Cars

"This time we were seriously out to make a record."
— Ric Ocasek

The winter of 1976 found the Cars holed up in Ric Ocasek's basement, working and reworking the collection of songs that would land them a record deal with Elektra/Asylum the following December and a passionate following in their home town, Boston. It was the winter that saw rock change, and probably change forever. The new music had become a new business — a *big* new business — but mostly in England. Punk was being processed through magazines, fanzines and burgeoning little record companies. It had hit the boutiques where you could spend a minor fortune buying the latest nifty designer-torn tee-shirt, multi-zippered jackets, and the current leather bondage items. For Malcolm McLaren, the Sex Pistols' manager and, in part, the architect of the brave new world of rock 'n' roll, punk wasn't for real; "It was just style." Exactly. And it was blasting a hole in the music industry and the new bands — the new pop bands — were walking through it.

There was still something called rock, of course. It was everything from "Leftoverture" by Kansas to Bob Seger's "Night Moves" to "Fly Like an Eagle" by the Steve Miller Band, all top sellers of the time. Just to let you know how truly odd-ball everything was, Debby Boone's "You Light Up My Life" and Barry Manilow's "Weekend in New England" were also top-selling records. Record sales exceeded the three billion dollar mark for the first time, on the way to the music industry's biggest boom — and biggest bust. The Rolling Stones signed a six-year pact which could bring them up to $21 million. Rock was rolling in it — except, that is, for the new generation of bands.

But very noticeably, the very word "rock" was beginning to lose some of its luster. Punk, new wave, no wave, non-wave — the very bands these terms characterized were making deliberately sure that everyone knew what their style *wasn't.* And what it wasn't simply was like what had come before.

The Guilford Stranglers, later just the Stranglers, borrowed from the past, particularly from the Doors, but there was little doubt that they weren't about nostalgia. The Jam were neo-Mod, today's Who, but they did bring a brand-new spirit. Tom Robinson and the Clash, the Boomtown Rats and Elvis Costello were all hitting their stride in Britain but were being carried on only a few Boston radio stations when the Cars made their debut on New Year's Eve, 1976, at Pease Air Force Base in New Hampshire. But there was an enormous gap between the new music and the new music industry and, if anything, it looked as though the gap was widening, especially in America. Television, the shortlived New York band with Tom Verlaine, had two hit singles in England but was ignored in North America. Talking Heads sold enough to make it on to some hit

OVERLEAF: The Cars in London, Ontario.

24

ABOVE: Ben with the tour bus driver.
OPPOSITE TOP: The Cars pose with The Romantics.
OPPOSITE BOTTOM: The Cars with Steve Berkowitz and Kim Cook from WEA
Canada.

parade charts but were also mostly ignored by radio. Disco was everywhere. What was wanted, particularly in America, was a band with new ideas but which managed to embrace enough of rock's mainstream ideas to gain acceptance.

Well, all that needed to be done at the time was to listen to a new song by this band out of Boston. It's called "Good Times Roll," but as its writer, the lean Ric Ocasek, explains, "It's not really about 'good times' at all. It begins with a droll and lagging guitar riff that sets a tempo that's almost *too* slow. That's all in one stereo channel. In the other, there's an out-of-synch electronic blip that beats like an oscillator pulse. Then, in the middle, there's a voice, a dry, straining and somewhat distant voice suggesting that we all should let the good times roll."

Great — it's party time, right? Forget it. Let the mega-stadium bands get your juices pumping with screams of "Partyyyyyyy!!!!" The Cars are dealing with consequences, here. These good times will knock you around. You could look a little foolish.

But suddenly, though, the music relents and the various rhythms all coalesce into a fundamental rock and roll format that builds in power to...what's that? The words "good times roll" are being sung in a distinctly familiar style. *Very* familiar. As in *Beatles* familiar. The Beatles. The Beatles? Jeez. Here, on the first cut on the very first album by a brand-new band, is the hook. And there, being reeled in by something that hits home, are all the deejays across America, desperate for something new to play, something *good* and by an American band — but something that doesn't sound like it comes from another planet, like England for instance. Like, hey Brucie, catch this. Like it? Yeah, me too. It's by a band called the Cars.

It wasn't "Good Times Roll" but another song, "Just What I Needed," that became the most requested piece around Boston's alternative rock shows. The band played as often as it could around town during the early part of 1977. They were on their own, familiar enough faces having appeared around Boston in other bands before — in some cases, even together before. But this time out

Flying to New Orleans.
David, Elliot, and Ben (front
row). Co-manager Steve
Berkowitz, Greg and Ric (back
row).

they were approaching it differently. They'd been burned before. They'd expected the record industry to come to them. This time they decided to go to it. They'd decided, as Ocasek explains, "to go out and get it instead of waiting for it to come to us. This time, we were seriously out to make a record."

The band went from opening-act status to headline status while making the rounds of such clubs as Don Law's 550-seat The Paradise. They were news. Their first manager, Fred Lewis, one-time road manager for the J. Geils Band, had first heard them when an early edition of the band was called Cap'n Swing. Cap'n Swing had recorded a demo and a pair of songs; "Strawberry Moonlight" and "Come Back Down" were being played locally. If not exactly hot, the band was at least warm, with critics picking up on its Roxy Music references and its Velvet Underground tones. Lewis knew he was on to something and he in turn urged Don Law, a Boston promoter, to take notice. In short notice the band had a break — a chance to open for Bob Seger at the 4,800-seat Music Hall. The band was somewhat unprepared for the gig and Greg Hawkes had to drive in at the last moment from Baltimore. But they were a hit and were given a standing ovation. What was even a bigger hit for them was "Just What I Needed," which was getting even more local airplay than their Cap'n Swing songs. When the Cars opened for Rick Derringer at The Paradise, the local crowd was already treating it like a hit, asking for it from beginning to end of their set.

Major labels weren't unaware of the Cars by now, and several record company executives came snooping around. Here was an unsigned band and already there were Cars buttons on the market. To complicate matters even more, the industry guys kept hearing about a single that BCN and Coz — that's WBCN-FM and WCOZ-FM — were playing, and playing *a lot*. Damned if they weren't playing that single more than they were playing the big hits. Here was a real movement, and it was all about a band no record company was making a red cent on.

Elektra Records was a bit more risk-taking than other labels and signed the band in December 1977. The concerted Cars' effort had paid off although, at the time, they would have been happy with even modest record sales. Getting the deal had meant something. Being scouted by a veteran producer, Roy Thomas Baker, meant something else again. They'd thought about having others produce them — John Lennon was one possibility. But they liked Baker's work. Besides, he had struggled through a blizzard to catch the band at a South Massachusetts high school, and the Cars liked the interest he showed in them. The band wanted to record immediately; they also wanted to record in England. Baker was agreeable to both ideas. A deal was struck. In January 1978, the band was in London and a month later their debut album was finished. *The Cars* was released in May. The first single, "Just What I Needed," was released a week before the album.

They had a hit on their hands. By October 1978, the single had sold over one million copies and the second single, "My Best Friend's Girl," came out to boost the LP even more. Not a band to waste their time, they toured Europe — England, France, Holland and Germany — by way of Belgium. Best of all, they found they had a hit in England. The next single, "Good Times Roll," arrived in 1979 shortly before the band headed back into the studio with Baker again, but in Los Angeles this time. By now the world was catching up to them. Most of the magazines that mattered — *Rolling Stone, Creem, Crawdaddy, Performance* and *Circus* — had identified the Cars as *the* band to watch. Even the Grammys recognized the new music and nominated the Cars among the Best New Artists of 1978.

And *The Cars* continued to sell. And sell. And sell. In fact *Candy-O*, the follow-up album, a crucial one for clues to the band's direction, was delayed because the first album wasn't flagging on the charts. By now, *The Cars* had sold more than two million copies and radio was convinced. And with reason; the Cars are accessible, not just musically but personally. The band had appeared not long after the release of their first album on "The Midnight Special" in 1978. The following year they were hosting the show and brought on their own favorite new band — at least Ric Ocasek's favorite new band, Suicide — to open for them. The Bee Gees were still fresh in America's mind when there, on coast-to-coast TV, was the band their mentor, Ocasek, knew would churn up a strong response.

"Everybody gets violently angry at Suicide," he said at the time, "which is the reaction they intend to get. The point is to express hatred without feeling guilty about it — to be loose about feeling angry."

The Cars, friends tell me, picked their name after they decided they liked it and had conducted a modest poll which confirmed that it was the very name they should have. It might not be terribly romantic but then again the Cars' history is not that kind of rock and roll romantic saga.

This is not to say they didn't go through it early on. They did. There were more than a few times which brought the band perilously close to packing it in. There were more than a few times when folks out there were willing to help them pack it in. The Cars met with active resistance at times and indifference at other times. One major company passed on the act in its early days because the

Looking cool in Houston.

A&R biggie who was brought to the club said "they have no presence."
Another passed, saying he "couldn't figure out the words."

It has never been easy for the Cars. But their struggle has been of a different kind from those of earlier bands. It's been one of problem solving as much as waiting. The Cars aren't a band that waits.

4 Style In Motion

"Three things about the Cars impress you immediately," wrote Michael Howell in *What's New*, early in 1978, barely a year after the band was formed. "One is that they are in total control of the situation: they're writing and playing music that really excites them, they respect and enjoy one another on- and offstage, they have a long-term contract with a major label [Elektra] and they are confident about the future."

By my count that's already five ways the Cars have impressed Howell. He gets to two more: the band's lack of compromises and the "effortless" manner with which they have handled all of the above. This may make the band sound rather like a Boy Scout troop, but you get the drift.

Here was a band arriving at what will likely be remembered as the most scrambled time (the late 70s) in rock's history, when there wasn't a name you could pin on the stuff; it was changing that fast. But the critics had already fixed on something crucial in the band's make-up. Call it the Car process; it's a view not of results but how things are done.

"Best in Calculation and Contrivance" went a headline in the *Vancouver Free Press*.

Early on, Ocasek had a ready answer for what they were up to; the Cars, he'd say, want to make rock "interesting." But if there ever was a loaded answer, this was it. What it was about them that attracted — "befuddled," perhaps, is a better word — critics was the different aspects of the Cars' sound. Put simply, no one could quite figure it out.

Greg Hawkes had made the distinction between rock and pop. The Cars were a pop band, he explained, because "we're song-oriented. The songs are made much simpler, much more to the point."

The Cars are very happy to use vitality where they find it, like in the pop song; the Cars charged up the pop song. "My Best Friend's Girl," Ocasek noted, put the classic pop-song yarn about the one-night stand "in a slightly different perspective." But this different perspective was worked out within the familiar form. The Cars weren't about to stretch the song form but they do celebrate the pop song the way Elvis Costello has been celebrating it. And the energy unleashed through this discovery has been enormous. The forms it took were enormous, too, as bands began to shape themselves in accord with the pop they played. The idea of pop in art embraced a variety of styles and notions — neo-Dada and New Realism. In music it became the Ramones and Television...and dozens of others.

But there's a knowing quality to this discovery. The Cars experimented.

They patched together inputs from various sources. They melded styles. They did just about anything and everything possible to underline Ocasek's lyrics and amplify their meaning. The Cars may have been new to all this; they never were naive. Ocasek's fascination with Andy Warhol is telling. Warhol was pop's great naive. ("Do you know what you are doing?" he was asked. "No," he said.) At least this was his stance, but his work — a constant critique of his life and times — would seem to show otherwise. The Cars' songs are also criticism. They're as much *about* pop as they *are* pop. "It's a sticky contradiction," Ocasek wrote. "It's a thing you call creation."

"If the Cars satirize, mock and trivialize pop, they embrace it and celebrate it too," said Mitchell Schneider in a review of the Cars. They were pop, punk and art-rock all rolled into one. "Though the sound is calculated and controlled, it has an enormous degree of freedom and casualness." James Isaac, in mid-summer 1977, was on to the same thing. Their image, he felt, "offers a number of intriguing dichotomies. There is in the band's material a recurring juxtaposition between 'poetic' lyrics and a style of rock and roll that relies heavily on a 'tinker toy sound.' "

Rolling Stone thought they might be the American Roxy Music. A *Los Angeles Times* review suggested Ocasek's "mannered vocals and nubbed-out lyrics of love in the modern world recall Bryan Ferry," while *High Fidelity* figured the Cars were the "first intellectual garage band."

Creem figured the Cars were "at once both *très outré* and rootie kazootie accessible." The *Christian Science Monitor*, as might be expected, looked for its set of references in more mainstream music. "There are faint traces of the Beatles, vague echoes of Queen, more distinct similarities to Bryan Ferry and Roxy Music, an underlying affinity with the Kinks, a brief aside to the early, ethereal days of King Crimson and more recent references to the thunderous power produced by the band Boston."

One-time Queen producer Roy Thomas Baker's name on the credits often produced the critical argument about how much he did — or didn't — contribute. Baker hadn't been picked because of his track record, Ocasek explained at the time. It wasn't because of Queen. The Cars liked his work with the Zombies and Free — bright, intelligent, heavy pop groups. "We decided to work with him because of his wonderful rapport with electronics and people. He respected our material and arrangements and wouldn't hesitate to try anything we wanted. Roy was responsible for the technical end of things and the atmosphere in the studio." *Scene* magazine in Ohio, although feeling that Baker maybe had "taken the Cars for a ride," nevertheless had to account (in a review that nearly over-dosed on automotive imagery) for the sheer variety in the music. *Pop Top* figured Baker had "imparted a glossy sheen to the material."

New Times, in the words of Jim Miller, found the Cars to be "a pop version of Roxy Music, redesigned by American kids to play in Peoria and sell to Led Zeppelin fans." He felt *The Cars* was the most forceful debut album since the arrival of the Sex Pistols.

At Pine Knob near Detroit.

5 Ben Orr

"When the band first got together, we had the idea we were just going to do our own kind of music and we were going to be as avant-garde as we thought we could be. We never counted on selling records in the millions."

Ben Orr

Bands aren't collectives, no matter what's said. Oh, maybe some things — money even — might be shared equally. But consensus has little to do with the way they work. Dynamics, on the other hand, do have a *lot* to do with it. Somewhere in the heart of a great rock 'n' roll band there's an essential contrast of styles and wills at work; Jagger and Richards with the Rolling Stones, Lennon and McCartney with the Beatles. With the Cars, a primary dynamic is between Ocasek and Orr, a dynamic that was at work even before the Cars became a band.

Their looks tell part of the story. Ocasek could be the young college prof: lean face, gaunt almost, somehow always slightly distant. Then there's Orr. There's no mistaking him. The rock 'n' roller. The front man. The lead singer. He's the one you notice first and not just because of his blond good looks but because he has something about him that asks to be noticed. Had he been born fifty years ago, he probably would have ended up in vaudeville. As it was, he ended up early in the Cleveland rock and roll scene which some might suggest is as close to vaudeville as rock gets. That's where Ocasek met him. Orr — then Ben Orzechowski — was a big star around Cleveland a way back. He led the house band on a local TV show but was not content to let it go at that so he did some session work. He was immediately attracted to Ocasek's early songs, and the two spent days just jamming together. Within a week or so, they'd formed their first band.

"At the beginning all we wanted was a record contract," says Orr. "It was just what every new group was hoping to get. We just wanted that record contract so we could put our music out — so that Ric could put his music out. It was real basic. You know, you grow up and you did cover songs, pretty much of what was popular back in the early days when you were in your teens. You did the hits. And you'd do the song even if you didn't particularly care about the lyrics.

"The process just carried over when you *did* care about the lyrics. It was a natural process. Ric's lyrics were just there. They needed to be done the way they were done; you just had to search for ways to put the lyrics across. I really don't know about the esthetic value of Ric's lyrics. I don't need to know. That's not what they're there for, y'know.

"Sometimes, with the way he writes, you're conscious about doing a lyric in a particular way. At times it just comes off so naturally you don't have to even think about it. It just sort of comes out of your mouth. It just flows. 'Drive' was that kind of natural thing. We heard the song on tape and he said, 'Do you

"When the time's ripe we get together; we just do it."

Ben Orr

want to try it?' I said, 'Yeah.' So I went out there and tried it and it just came off. We really didn't have to think about it. It happened right there. That's the really weird thing about it; it was one of the easiest ones.''

He thinks of "Drive's" aching but not sentimental tone as "lush, not wet." It wasn't nearly as planned as it may even sound. In fact the rockers on *Heartbeat City* were, according to Ben, "probably harder to do than 'Drive.' It flowed. And when we sat down and tried to figure out the order — verse, chorus, verse, chorus — that kind of thing — it came easily. It took the least amount of time. The only thing that did take time was the background vocals, getting that full-voiced sound. Other than that it was real easy, probably the easiest one we've done. A fluke.

"We generally deliberate about what we do. Ric comes to the studio with a general idea about material and sets in motion what he wants to start. Whatever basic tapes he has, he plays for us. He's got the general idea and we sit down and try to make it the best we can. So it is deliberate. It certainly doesn't happen by accident."

And this is a band that plans, he adds. "You have to, otherwise you can really run into a lot of trouble if things don't go exactly as they should. Before a tour, if you don't sit down with your lighting designer and set designer you might have equipment that is too big to get into the buildings you're playing. And with a coliseum or stadium, you can run into a lot of money problems. You can run into union problems — all kinds of problems. You can run into travel problems because the trucks can't get someplace. So everything's got to be planned out. And I think with us everybody does the best they can. The Michael Jackson Tour didn't work out too well because it didn't have very good planning.

"We're a band that has meetings. Do we have meetings! When it's work time we sit around and get right on top of everything we need to know. We *know* what's going on. Assistants? Assistants? We're just five guys running around. There are people who help us out in the studio but when we leave there, we're just normal people — almost."

In talking about *Heartbeat City,* Orr says, "It was probably the most precise album we've ever done. And I liked doing it the way we did it although I'm not sure if everyone in the group feels the same about it. We took hours getting certain parts just right at one point. That's why it took six months to finish the album. Each individual had to keep plugging away. Mutt Lange would hear the idea and then, if it was needed, we'd do three, maybe four more tracks on top of that one track. It was *that* precise. Every note had to be 'spot on,' as they say. So it did take a long time, but it was precise."

The trick is still to make it sound natural, he says. "If Bob Dylan wants to sound natural, he wants to do something one time and one time only. He wants to just sit down there and do it, and that's that. Our music sounds as if we came in just once and did it right, too, even though it can be really thick."

But *Heartbeat*'s rock direction — its tone colors beaming extra bright, its moods so well delineated — was not left to chance. The band had nudged it in this direction. "Everyone wants to have a record on the charts, one that's doing well," he says. "Everyone wants a record that has more people listening to it, one that draws different age groups. We'd pretty much got the pop part of what we do down. We'd already shown we can do the underground ideas. So this time around, for *Heartbeat,* we figured we'd make a little change and kind of keep it a straight-ahead rock'n'roll kind of record.

"But it's always been pop music, hasn't it? I guess at first we sounded different because we had a certain kind of rhythm section. People weren't used to our rhythm sound — that eight-beat *doonk-doonk-doonk* kind of thing with the

OPPOSITE: Ben barbecuing at home in Boston.

50

bass and drum really chunking away. *Doonk-doonk-doonk.* That's what made the sound. People weren't used to it, so they put it in a category that they could understand. But it was really just basic.

"When the band first got together, we had the idea we were just going to do our own kind of music and we were going to be as avant-garde as we thought we could be. We never counted on selling records in the millions. We figured, back in those days, that if we sold maybe 50,000 records it would be great for us. We had no idea as to where it would go or how large it would turn out. We kept pretty level-headed about it and figured maybe we'd sell 50,000 records. Okay, maybe 20,000 to 100,000 max. That was good enough for us then.

"Ric just wanted to have his music out there and we wanted to put together a really good band to perform it. So that's what we were doing at first — just a rock'n'roll band trying our best to do our best. And trying to enjoy what we were doing. I guess if nobody enjoyed it we wouldn't have done it in the first place. We were just after that record contract, you see; what every new group hopes to get starting out."

OPPOSITE: Elliot and Ben in Dallas.

BELOW: Flying to Dallas. Elliot, Ben and Ric (front); Steve Berkowitz (background).

Ben and his other passions — cars and bikes.

Ironically, each individual in the band is starting out again with a solo effort of one kind or another. "And it's a real good outlet for us," Ben says. "There are a lot of things you feel like doing after you've been out on the road. And doing something on your own is a good chance to blow off steam, musically. Everybody's having a good time. *I'm* certainly having a good time.

"When I'm doing my own recording, I figure it's just me. It doesn't sound like the Cars. Writing for the band right now is pretty much Ric's thing. My stuff doesn't sound like Ric's either. I don't try to write like Ric. I like writing about love and things that I expect and things that I see. Things that I've felt. Things that I want. I just put down what's inside of me. I try not to think about it too much.

"Now, as to recording my songs, the mechanics are pretty much the same as when we record the Cars. You get in the studio, you figure out a pattern you want — verse, chorus, verse, chorus — something like that. You put down a basic guitar track to sing to. You do a rough vocal based on that. And then you start sweetening. So it's just about the same as the Cars except the ideas are different because they're coming from a different place."

It's this ability to be independent that can keep the band together, he feels. "Before we recorded *Heartbeat City*, we were off about a year and a half — almost two years. And when everyone wanted to get together, we decided to do it. I imagine we still like each other a whole lot; we just do it. So I don't imagine any problems coming from these solo things. The only thing I can imagine happening is that if somebody's album is a real big hit, some Cars' thing may have to be put off because of someone's tour. That might postpone things. It won't mean that we don't want to play together again.

"We see each other. We bump into each other down at the studio. Yeah, we run into each other and that's nice."

OVERLEAF: Onstage in Worcester.

Ben with a roadie at Toronto's
Exhibition Stadium.

6 Setting The Pace

Candy-O, the Cars' second album, extended the electronics of the first; "Shoo Be Doo" notably is awash with gentle electronics. It also extended *Candy-O*'s gimlet-eyed view of the world. Once again, the Cars present a world in which things aren't quite as nice and easy as you want them to be. Take care, the Cars are saying. You can get what you want. It may even be what you need. But once you have it, you want something new again.

Its bright, peppy cover aside, *Candy-O* was a darker album than the first. But that didn't stop it from zipping up the charts, selling more than a million copies in a mere two months. With the band's albums no longer competing with one another, the record company released a series of singles: "Let's Go" with "That's It" on the flip side arrived first in June 1979; "It's All I Can Do" backed by "Got A Lot On My Head" came out in September of that same year; and "Double Life" with "Candy-O" on the flip side was released in December.

Then the band took its first break since signing the record deal. Each member went about the rest of his life: Easton, working with the bright young guitar builder, Dean Zelinsky, developed his own custom-designed guitars; Robinson designed the cover for the upcoming *Panorama* album; Greg composed and Ric produced a variety of demos as well as recording an album for Suicide at the Power Station in New York (where the band would record *Panorama* in part). Ben Orr wasn't quite as lucky. His apartment was swept away in the flames that destroyed the building he was living in, and he had to settle somewhere else.

It was what they *didn't* do that was as startling as anything they did at this point in their history— they didn't leave Boston. The local Boston scene had picked up the spirit of the new music as fast as, if not faster than, most cities, and by the time the Cars had become the city's new heavy-hitting act (with all due respect to Boston and Aerosmith), local clubs were hearing the likes of the Peter Dayton Band, Artyard, CCCP-TV and Mission of Burma. A few of these bands were given a chance to play to an audience that otherwise would have never heard them — or heard of them — until the Cars began to use local acts to open their shows at Boston Garden.

"But it wasn't just that they didn't leave town; they remained really active around town," says one local critic. "A famous act can stay at home and still move to Hollywood – in its thinking. The Cars didn't do that. They still haven't. They bought a studio here (Intermedia, which they renamed Syncro Sound), and they can be seen around here. They can be found hanging out in the local clubs

OPPOSITE: Ben (on keyboard) and Elliot in Houston.

''But the high point was the heart in all this techno-wizardry. The high point was Ben Orr singing 'Drive.' ''

sometimes. That may not do anything for record sales, but it sure makes an impression on the city.''

Panorama, produced by Roy Thomas Baker, is perhaps the most adventurous of all Cars albums; it was released in mid-summer of 1980, in time for the band's mammoth tour. ''Touch and Go'' was the first single off it (backed by ''Down Boys''). Released in August, it was followed in November by ''Don't Tell Me No'' with ''Don't Go To Pieces'' on the flip side.

The Cars weren't working at the pace most bands worked at. They were working faster. They'd revved up their development. *Panorama* was reflective to the degree that it seemed to survey everything that had happened to the band up to that point — all the tours, the success. It embraced what the band felt was its present musical status. The Cars were in a hurry to get on with their history.

Well, it was a hit — selling somewhere over a million copies — but it wasn't the hit the band had hoped for. The next album, *Shake It Up*, was closer in spirit to *Candy-O*, although somehow sweeter.

From the start, they'd walked the line between hot-selling top-40, get-on-with-it radio pop and its more experimental developments. *Panorama* took a step beyond this line; *Shake It Up* took a step back to the middle. *Heartbeat City* was another step away, but this time the experiment was of a different sort. The Cars, so it seems, had come to realize that whatever else their albums were, they were great collections of songs. Their critics had come to realize that this wasn't a bad thing at all. Their audience, of course, had known this all along.

The pop song was rediscovered by some in the late 70s, and by the mass audience in the mid-80s. Obviously, pop musicians had always been writing pop songs, but it took a generation that included Ric Ocasek, Elvis Costello and Cyndi Lauper to realize that writing songs for radio, and hence for a mass audience, wasn't in itself limiting — that it could be enormously liberating. What resulted was one of the most remarkable turnarounds in music history, a period of pop to rival rock's halcyon days of the late 50s and mid-60s. And right in the middle of it, preparing a sad-eyed ballad called ''Drive'' which was about a guy wondering how his girl was going to get home, were the Cars.

Rock, despite its immediacy, always seems to sound best when it rolls through our memories. One generation remembers rock's first golden age of the late 50s. Another remembers its second golden age of the mid-60s. Elvis and the Beatles.

What the Cars' success as a singles — as well as an album — band points to is that they've been operating at their peak period in the peak period of pop.

And it has to do with all of pop's deceptively simple surface qualities, its brightness and immediacy. What made the pop song so appealing today is what made it appealing in 1958 or 1967 — to point to two top years in pop's top periods — its seemingly instant response to the very mood and tone of the day you hear it.

There's nothing in a lot of what you pick up on the charts these days that demands to be remembered. Then again, there were such artistically inflated hopes behind ''All I Have To Do Is Dream'' by the Everly Brothers back in 1958, or Bobby Gentry's ''Ode To Billy Joe'' in 1967. But often it's the less obvious or less demanding that's most remembered: the sheer sadness in Ben Orr's voice when he sings ''Who's going to take you home, tonight''; Chet Atkins' ringing guitar chords on the Everly Brothers' hit; or the sultry heat oozing out of Gentry's mystery ballad.

Let's admit from the outset that this is all rather subjective. Who's to say that 1978 wasn't a great year for pop, too, with the Bee Gees and *Saturday*

Night Fever being heard everywhere and seemingly all at once? Well, as it turned out, a lot of people said it — those who hated the dominance of disco.

Shake It Up and *Heartbeat City* were both reservoirs for singles. From the former came ''Since You're Gone'' backed with ''Think It Over'' released in March 1982. From the latter came ''You Might Think'' with ''Heartbeat City'' on the flip side, early in 1984. Then followed the hit ''Magic'' in May of '84; ''Drive'' arrived in July of the same year and was to dominate the charts until the fall; then ''Hello Again'' in October and, finally, ''Why Can't I Have You'' in January 1985, backed with a song that wasn't on the *Heartbeat City* album, ''Breakaway.''

Few albums in recent pop history, even movie-album soundtrack compilations, were so continuously heard during the course of a year. More than that, the sheer variety in this list of songs is remarkable. What's even more remarkable is that the variety didn't bother radio programmers.

And it might have; at one time, when each station had its own format, if you didn't fit you weren't played. But the new pop hammered away at radio for so long that radio had to give in. Suddenly it was responsive to change, and variety and changes-of-pace — everything the Cars had been about for years. Radio had caught up with them. ''Two years ago radio wouldn't play a song, no matter how good it was, if an artist didn't suit the radio station's image,'' says one particular manager. ''Now image doesn't matter.''

The Cars helped force this change mainly because they had the right image (tough, mysterious guys who play loud) even if their music didn't suit the image rock radio had of them.

Video helped kick radio out of its complacency and booted pop into gear. It offered such a dizzying variety of styles and images that radio just had to yield. And the Cars' videos were among the most challenging and elegant of the lot because there was no consistent ''Cars look.'' Each video went in its own direction, now high-tech and very modern, now direct and action-filled.

But other factors were involved in the pop song's comeback: the new generation of pop stars, particularly women; the impact of black music on every kind of pop; the importance of the pop song and the single over the concept piece and the album; and money.

That's money as in *big* money. By 1984, 131 albums had sold more than 500,000 copies in the United States according to the Recording Industry Association of America (RIAA), and fifty-nine other albums had sold one million copies each; 109 more albums had sold anywhere from two million copies and up. In 1958, the first year the RIAA started rating gold records, there was only one gold album (the *Oklahoma* original soundtrack) and four gold singles: Perry Como's ''Catch A Falling Star''; Laurie London's ''He's Got The Whole World''; Perez Prado's ''Patricia''; and Elvis Presley's ''Hard-Headed Woman.''

The money and statistics generated by this economic dynamo aren't the only ways of measuring the quality of today's pop — or yesterday's.

Even in the very teeth of pop's period of High Seriousness in 1967, with everyone taking the Beatles, psychedelia and flowers in their hair very seriously indeed, there was a bevy of pop tunes which are now sounding better and better as psychedelia is sounding sillier and sillier. The year when the concept album was at its peak also produced a list of top sellers with the Young Rascal's ''Groovin' ''; ''The Letter'' by the Box Tops; ''Light My Fire'' by the Doors; and ''I'm A Believer'' by the Monkees.

The same applies right now. The success of ''Drive'' goes way beyond its multi-million sales. It was a great single among other great singles, a glitter of gold in a golden age of pop.

The Cars' 1984 tour to support the new album was perhaps the most technologically honed tour in the band's history. Its sound was vast, enormous — stretching the acoustics of each stadium to its limits. It was also a reunion of sorts, with Ocasek back from recording his own solo album for Gerren Records. And the band paraded its history, going back to "Just What I Needed." "But the high point," wrote one critic, "was the heart in all this techno-wizardry. The high point was Ben Orr singing 'Drive.'"

7 Greg Hawkes

To understand something about Greg Hawkes, you need to know that he likes Frank Zappa — not just *all* of Frank Zappa, but in particular the more classical Zappa. He has the collection of Zappa pieces conducted by Boulez. He likes Zappa's synthesized version of the contemporary of Mozart, Francesco Zappa. To be sure, Hawkes' interests don't start or stop there. He's collected German auto-electro music and has listened to New York-based classical minimalist Philip Glass. If there's an intellectual thread that runs through all of this — and you can add to the heady mix science fiction in all its forms — it's this: a fascination with the kind of experimental art that is actually practiced, music that's just this side of being a musical guerrilla attack. He grew up listening to early Zappa, "the 'Uncle Meat,' 'Burnt Weanie Sandwich,' 'Hot Rats,' period" he tells me. But it's the direction of the more recent Zappa, he adds, that points to the direction he'd like some of his own, private music to go in: "I'm writing some stuff of my own as well, and I'm looking to do a solo project with it."

As with the others, he's also developed a strong visual sense. "The albums' covers," he says, "have really been David's work. They're very important. But for me, too, the whole idea of graphic image is really important and I spend a lot of time with my own drawings. I'm doing them all on computer these days. I've got an Apple II and a couple of software programs and I'm teaching myself computer animation. I've got a couple of little characters walking back and forth across the screen. My interest in comic books comes from reading them as a kid — and as an adult. I must have a few thousand at home. Strangely enough, I haven't really been following them these days because I don't think there's much interest in the field right now."

But maybe the comic books provide a kind of anchor, especially when it comes to music-making. "Hopefully, I'd like to retain some sense of goofiness and not take it all too seriously," he goes on. "I think if you approach it with the idea, 'Okay, we've got to make some art now,' that it's going to end up being a little stuffy or pretentious or something."

In a sense, the Cars' balancing act between pure pop and pop-art is Hawkes' own. Ric and Ben met him in 1974; they'd been in Boston for more than a year, and he'd been playing around town after moving to Boston from Baltimore. "They had been together for three or four shows as the Cars before I joined," he recalls. "In fact, I heard them as the Cars sometime in January 1977." Hawkes played a broad range of reed instruments too, but Ocasek had

OPPOSITE: Greg at home, working on the computer.

Boston TV crew shooting Elliot for a show.

vironments for our songs to flourish in. Once we're done with a record, the writers try to figure out what to call it or what to make of it, and music fans and listeners decide whether they like it or not. If enough of them do like it, then it becomes commercial music.

"But while we're recording it we're not thinking about any of that, really. We're not saying, 'Okay, well, this is a hit and this is the B-side.' We just record songs. We try to make records as well as we can. We use our own artistic sensibilities to set the parameters.

"At the time of the group's inception we had a concept in mind. We had an idea of a pop band that was more than just 'Hello My Bluebird' or whatever. But, at the same time, we all grew up loving top-40 radio and the music we grew up with.

"We'd grown up the product of our times and our music is a reflection of that. We never sat down and said, 'Well, we're going to be a hard rock band.' We were just being us.

"In the studio, sometimes things develop that aren't expected or an idea might pop up that might change direction of a song once we're well into the recording of it. It's never black and white. There are no hard and fast rules, which is one of the nice things about the band. Generally, for past albums, we've rehearsed extensively for the album's songs and gone in and more or less laid tracks down according to what we had rehearsed. Working with Mutt Lange on *Heartbeat City* was a little bit different because we did all the pre-production work with him. He was involved at the same time as the other members of the band, which is to say that we weren't coming to him with all these songs already rehearsed. It was a different process from the first four albums."

Indeed, what was expected to be a two-month stay in London, where *Heartbeat City* was recorded, turned out to last six months. In going from Roy Thomas Baker to Mutt Lange, the Cars had gone from a producer who treated

Elliot waiting for the band's manager, Elliott Roberts.

rock and roll as *sturm und drang,* full of sudden dramatic shifts in volume, tone, mood and texture, to a producer who carefully crafted huge structures detail by detail — a modern medieval architect. And I wondered out loud to Easton if he felt some spontaneity had been lost in the process. John Lennon — someone the band had thought about to produce their debut album — felt constrained after so many crafted Beatles albums. Could a band operate successfully for the Hit Parade and still be truly immediate?

Weeks after we'd talked, I ended up on the phone one night with Elliot Easton. He's been worried, he tells me, about all the references to the Beatles. "It sounds a bit pompous to put yourself next in the chain of influence from Elvis to Beatles in saying that maybe kids will want to be a Car," he adds. "It seems a little bit weird."

"I understand," I tell him, "but don't you think that's possible — that there are kids out there maybe they heard the band at the Live Aid concert [in Philadelphia, on July 13, '85] who want to be Cars?"

"Well," he said, "maybe for a few kids, our albums might be the thing to make them want to play guitar. But I don't think there'll be anything of the magnitude of the former groups that we've mentioned. When I thought about it, I thought, well, maybe it might be true if it were Van Halen or Culture Club or Duran Duran. I think those groups have more kid appeal than the Cars. I'm sure there's a lot of kids in our audience, but there's more of a balance than, say, a heavy metal band or Michael Jackson."

"Where do you see the Cars' role in this?" I wondered.

"I can sort of get a handle on where I think we fit into the history of pop music," he continues. "I think basically we were part of a very exciting time in 1977 when music was changing a little and there was an interest in the excitement of rock and roll again after a long period of so-called progressive rock and there was a renewed interest in that energy. It was an exciting time. It was a time when some of the groups that became really great were playing in America and in London when everything was happening. I wouldn't say we were part of the punk movement by any stretch of the imagination. But maybe in our own way we were one of the early bands to get the energy of that across to a mass audience.

"You can't really feel the way I feel about it being a part of it. There's a lot of groups out there, Peter. I mean, the Cars are one of them and a great one. But I think the Cars have their own style and their own sound. And it's not

one particular sound but it always sounds like the Cars — you can recognize the band. And I think that's a great thing. Because it's terrible when you turn on the radio and every group sounds the same. But you've got to be careful about tooting your own horn because you can get an inflated view of what you're doing.''

"But," I say, "the success of those singles, and I don't mean just on the charts—"

"Rick writes the songs," he says. "Let's face it."

"Nonetheless, the band has released a remarkable string of singles in a period of remarkable singles."

"Well," he says, "it's funny, because we're always wrong about picking singles. Or a lot of times we're wrong. We'll have a song while we're making an album and it will be just everybody's favorite. And the record company will pick something else. Sometimes during the course of an album, we'll say 'Maybe that sounds like a strong single' or 'That's a contender.' But our thinking can change. We're just trying to make every song great — as good as we can. And then they pick the single with whatever science they have for doing it. But I think singles are great. Phil Spector — his whole arena was singles. He made little pocket symphonies. Albums did nothing to a guy like Spector. It was the records. The singles. I like that. It's nice to put everything into one song. The Beach Boys' 'Good Vibrations' — that one song took six months to record. You can really do something with a single."

He pauses, then adds: "I was going to use the Beatles again. It's easy to do. I just flashed 'Strawberry Fields' on the wall."

"But you guys went after that didn't you?" I asked. "To make great singles."

"No," he says, shortly. "We did say we were going to make our music concise and not have a lot of doodling and solos. We never did say we're going to be a hit single band. I mean, we probably would have laughed at something like that when we made our first record. We didn't know what it was going to become. And we were amazed when it first caught on the way it did.

"You don't really know. You never know. And when you think you do, you're in trouble. You just have to put everything you can into it and hope it goes over. As we both know, I'm sure you have heard albums that you thought were fantastic through the years and never did anything and you couldn't understand why. I guess a lot of it's timing.

"I think that maybe we came along at a time when people were sick of what they were being force-fed and were ready for a change.

"At the time that we went out on our first tours, people thought we were really weird in the Midwest and stuff and thought we were like punk music because they'd never seen anything like that, but it's all relative."

"We'd grown up a product of our times and our music is a reflection of that, really. We never sat down and said, 'Well, we're going to be a hard-rock band.' We were just being us."

Elliot Easton

9 David Robinson

"We just established a trust and an understanding about how we were going to approach the music and that made us confident enough to know that when we did start to play, the music would work out well."

David Robinson

There are those who'll tell you drummer David Robinson gave the band its focus. People like Maxanne Sartori, for instance; the ex-Boston WBCN deejay — more recently a music consultant for WNEW-FM in New York — hyped local acts and had picked up on the Cars right from the beginning.

"But they had no stage look," she says. "They couldn't afford a stage look. Plus they were the opening act for the first year so they really couldn't put anything on the stage other than themselves. But David came along and really changed the way they looked. A lot. I've got pictures of Ric playing in blue jeans. I mean, obviously they couldn't afford good clothes back then. Ben's wife used to sew all his clothes for him. The others sort of wore what they had. But David — I'd known him from the Modern Lovers, and I shared a house with him in 1971. David could have twenty-five cents in his pocket and look the best guy at the party. So I think David did a lot about the way the band looked.

"Musically, too. Musically, David straightened the band out, I would say. I think he made the whole impact of the band a lot straighter. It was very convoluted when I first saw it. It was very Steely Dan-ish. It was almost jazzy in some respects. They had a real jazzy bass player, a real jazzy drummer, you know, people who overplayed a lot. One of the things that David did was straighten out the whole format."

Robinson was one of the founding members of Jonathon Richman's Modern Lovers and stayed with them until the band went acoustic, thus rendering a percussionist unnecessary. After a stint with Pop!, a Los Angeles-based group, he found himself back in Boston playing with DMZ when Ocasek approached him.

"I could tell when I first met Ric," says Robinson, "before we even really played any music together, that he understood the value of having at least part of the music be in the spirit that the Modern Lovers' music was in.

"When we first got together, well, we didn't really talk specifically about music. Mostly it was just emotional and seeing what our backgrounds were. We talked about what we appreciated and what we didn't like; what we wanted to do and what we didn't like to do; and who we didn't like and who was around at the time, and why, and...yeah, it was mostly personal.

"We didn't sit down and say, 'Okay, when we start the group we'll do this song this way and this song that way.' We just established a trust and an understanding about how we were going to approach the music and that made us confident enough to know that when we did start to play, the music would work out well. We knew there wouldn't be any big surprises or that people's

OPPOSITE: David — getting ready backstage.

personalities would be way off from what we first imagined from our first impression."

If all of them are alike in any way it's that they approach being a Car in a rather low-key manner, he adds. "And I think that's the case because we plan things out very thoroughly. From the start we thought that if this was really going to be a chance to get somewhere, we'd better be careful. We knew that we'd all made lots of mistakes before and we learned from them.

"I remember in talking with Ric early on that things should be interesting; that we wouldn't play down to people with our music; and that you could strike a middle ground somewhere between what you thought was esthetically proper art and what was commercially acceptable to people.

"People have said that what we play is hard to peg. People aren't really sure if they want to call it art or coliseum rock. And it isn't either of those things. But that's kind of hard for people to believe. I guess it's a little bit of both those things, but it's mostly just unique."

If Robinson pushed the band toward a focused visual style, he's also given the band a nudge in a musical way. He senses how far the Cars have gone musically. "To me, all the songs on the *Heartbeat City* album sound very similar to me — they're all really full; they're somehow different from each other and yet the same in a way. But maybe there is a basic difference between this and the first album. All the songs on the first album sound like Cars songs. I mean, that was what they had in common. That was what made them sound similar to each other. But I think on *Heartbeat City* there's a little bit more of traditional pop styles in the songs.

"But then, *Heartbeat City* is so much producer Mutt Lange's album that, to be honest with you, I had little to do with the way it sounds. I wasn't really there when the songs were arranged and that's really where they take on their Cars-sounding quality, if there is such a thing. And I did all the drum parts last. Normally I would do a drum part and be in on everybody else's parts, listening and giving my opinion and just always being there to see what the direction is. But to do it backwards, it just limited my input so much that the songs had such a strong direction by the time I got to them, my influence was minor."

But this is the pragmatic way the Cars work. *Heartbeat City* — originally there was some thought to call it "Who'll Drive You Home" — was recorded in London. It took nearly a half-year to do, it required the band to live together in the same house, it forced them to learn new ways of recording — and it worked.

Right from the start, Robinson goes on, "I think we all really wanted to be commercially successful. As for the music, Ric brings the songs and we just pick the best ones. If he wrote twenty songs and fifteen of them were ballads, we would just pick the best ones. If it turned out to be an album with twelve ballads, we would do it. I'd guess you'd say Ric is really pretty much in charge of things now."

It's a system that works. "I'm not sure that if the Modern Lovers had stayed together," he goes on, "they ever would have been in sync with people's tastes—people who want to buy records, people who buy a lot of records. The Modern Lovers were always either just a little outside of what was going on or way ahead of what was going on. Then again, I think that if they ever had gotten in sync they wouldn't have been anywhere near as interesting. So they could probably have stayed together longer but never sold any records."

Robinson has his solo interests as well, producing an album for a local band at Syncro Sound.

Oh, he's heard the break-up rumors. (Sartori says that "David, Greg and Elliot would want to be Cars forever and ever. But Ric and Ben are gypsies.

They've had so many lives before. They've had other families. They've changed their looks. They could keep on changing.'')

Says David, ''Breaking up is another thing that's sort of in Ric's control. I know none of us wants to break it up — I certainly don't. If for some reason he felt the band wasn't the vehicle for his songs anymore, I assume he would break it up or leave it. But I don't see that happening; I mean, I don't see any reason why that should happen.

''As for the Cars going out on the road, well, that's Ric's thing. He hates to tour. He would rather not play any live gigs at all. So the decision to tour is pretty much a compromise between him not wanting to tour at all and other people realizing that we have to tour.

''I like it, personally. I wouldn't kill myself doing it eight months out of the year. But if there's enough work out there, and people won't see you without milking it, I think you should play.''

What Robinson is doing is going back to the beginnings — his own and, in a way, any rock band's. And in their individual ways, that's what the others are doing as well: Ric setting his words to music again; Elliot, with his first solo album out and tour finished; Ben with his in the works and Greg thinking about his. The Cars aren't coasting. The Cars are hearing the hum of the engine.

Discography

The Cars (Elektra 6E-135, 1978)
Good Times Roll, My Best Friend's Girl, Just What I Needed, I'm In Touch With Your World, Don't Cha Stop, You're All I've Got Tonight, Bye Bye Love, Moving In Stereo, All Mixed Up.

Candy-O (Elektra 5E-507, 1979)
Let's Go, Since I Held You, It's All I Can Do, Double Life, Shoo Be Doo, Candy-O, Night Spots, You Can't Hold On Too Long, Lust For Kicks, Got A Lot On My Head, Dangerous Type.

Panorama (Elektra 54-514, 1980)
Panorama, Touch and Go, Gimme Some Slack, Don't Tell Me No, Getting Through, Misfit Kid, Down Boy, You Wear Those Eyes, Running To You, Up and Down.

Shake It Up (Elektra 54-567, 1981)
Since You're Gone, Shake It Up, I'm Not the One, Victim of Love, Cruiser, A Dream Away, This Could Be Love, Think It Over, Maybe Baby.

Heartbeat City (Elektra 60-296, 1984)
Hello Again, Looking For Love, Magic, Drive, Stranger Eyes, You Might Think, It's Not The Night, Why Can't I Have You, I Refuse, Heartbeat City.

The Cars Greatest Hits (Elektra 96-4641, 1985)
Tonight She Comes, Just What I Needed, Since You're Gone, Good Times Roll, You Might Think, Touch and Go, Drive, My Best Friend's Girl, Heartbeat City, Let's Go, I'm Not The One, Magic, Shake It Up.

Philip Kamin began photographing rock bands in 1978 when he picked up a camera for the first time and asked Phil Collins, singer and drummer for Genesis, to go on their tour. Since the fall of 1982 Philip has photographed and/or written twenty-five internationally distributed books. His photographs have appeared worldwide in magazines, song books, programs, album covers and posters.

Along with award-winning writer Peter Goddard, Philip has produced two books on The Rolling Stones and The Cars and books on The Who, David Bowie, The Police, Genesis, Van Halen, Duran Duran, Michael Jackson and the Jacksons, Bruce Springsteen, Wham!, Phil Collins, David Lee Roth, Madonna, Bryan Adams, Tears for Fears, Paul Young, Howard Jones, Tina Turner, Cyndi Lauper, and Corey Hart.

Philip Kamin uses **Canon**™ cameras and equipment exclusively—bodies: F1, A1, T80, T70 and Sure Shot and Sure Shot bodies with motor drives; lenses: 24 mm f/2, 35 mm f/2, 50 mm f/1.4, 85 mm f/1.8, 135 mm f/2, 200mm f/2.8, 300 mm f/4 Aspherical, 400 mm f/4.5 and 600 mm f/4.5; and the **Canon**™ strobe system.

Peter Goddard is the rock and jazz critic of the *Toronto Star*. He has written for a variety of magazines in Canada, the U.S. and France, and has received a National Newspaper Award for critical writing. Goddard has an M.A. in music and a degree in solo piano performance. He has written several scores for experimental film, including electronic music, and has written and produced for television and radio. Peter, his wife and daughter reside in Toronto, and they spend part of the year on their farm in France. Peter is currently working on a novel, and has been commissioned to write a history of popular music.